Editions KINA ITALIA

Hyères

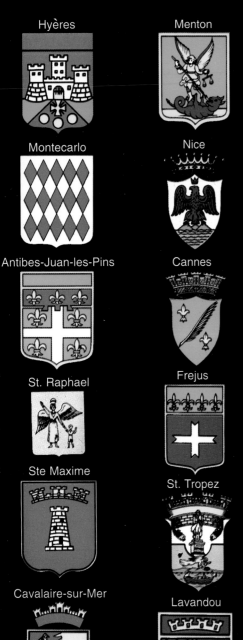

Menton

Montecarlo

Nice

Antibes-Juan-les-Pins

Cannes

St. Raphael

Frejus

Ste Maxime

St. Tropez

Cavalaire-sur-Mer

Lavandou

Toulon

Sanary-sur-Mer

Bandol

St.Rémy-de-P.
Cavaillon
Apt
Céreste
Volx
Valensole
Riez
Orgon
Bonnieux
Manosque
Gréoux-les-Bain
Quinson
Ste
Sénas
Grambois
Eyguières
Cadenet
Mirabeau
SALON
Pt-Royal
Durance
Pertuis
St.Paul
Ginasseris
Verdon
Montr
Lambesc
Peyrolles
La Verdière
Miramas
Coudoux
Meyrargues
Rians
St. Chamas
AIX-EN-P
Varagas
Tavernes
Istres
Berre
Rognac
Châteauneuf-le-R
Barjois
Les Milles
Ollié-es
Fos
Etang de Berre
Cabriès
Port-de-Bouc
Martigues
Gardanne
Trets
St.Maxim
la-S.te Baume
Le Val
Carce
Marignane
P.de Cuques
La Destrousse
Lavéra
Carry-le-Rouet
Le Logis - Tourves
de-Nans
Brignoles
MARSEILLE
Roquevaire
La Roquebrussanne
Besse
Château d'If
ubagne
La Ste Baume
Forcalqueire
Cap Croisette
Gémenos
Signes
Méounes
les-Montr.
Pu
Cassis
Le beausset
Solliès -Pont
Cuers
Pier
I. de Riou
La Ciotat
Les Lécques
TOULON
La
Bandol
Hyères
Sanary
I. des Embiez
La Seyne
St.Mandrier
Rad
Six Fours
Cap Sicié
Golfe de Giens
Gien
La
Porquerolles
Ile de Porqu

M   E   R   M

The Côte d'Azur, which encompasses the area between Menton and Hyères, is administratively part of the Maritime Alps département, but geographically it belongs to the Provence region, located in the southeast part of France. The beauty of the sea and the charm of the inland area, which became known as the Côte d'Azur only when the poet Stephen Liégeard coined it at the end of the 19th century, make this one of the most enchanting areas of the Mediterranean. Morphologically, the territory in this coastal region is not totally homogenous. While the first portion, Corniche de la Riviera, located between Menton and Nice, is characterized by an uneven landscape due to the rocky slopes of the mountainous buttresses inland that continue all the way to the sea, the area from Nice to Cannes is much more gentle, with a lower coastline dominated by numerous inlets edged by vast sandy beaches. Farther on, the Côte d'Azur once again becomes jagged and uneven, especially in the area between Cannes and Saint-Raphaël, known as Corniche de l'Esterel, famous for its tormented and fascinating appearance and for the red color of the rocks that plunge into the sea, and between Saint-Raphaël and Hyères, known as Corniche des Maures, dotted with inlets, bays, capes and small promontories traced by the final buttresses of the mountains that rise behind the coastal area. Characteristically Mediterranean flora (both native and introduced by human cultivation) flourishes throughout the entire coastal region, especially in the wilder areas which have not suffered from development. In particular, there are shrubs like thyme, rosemary, sage, laurel, marjoram, lavender and mimosa, as well as olive trees (imported here by the Greeks over two thousand years ago) and grapes (excellent wines are produced in the vineyards in the region) in the immediate inland area, along with plane trees, cypresses, almond trees and various varieties of oak and pine, from maritime species (cluster pines) to the Aleppo pine. In addition, encouraged by the particularly mild climate, various rare and exotic plants grow in the parks and gardens of urban areas (especially roses, jasmines, carnations, oranges, eucalyptus and succulents).

The sea, with its splendid crystalline color that gives the whole coast its name, is certainly the main attraction of the region, along with the sandy beaches characteristic of the Côte d'Azur. Those who prefer the lively bustle, brightness and animation of the more worldly and exclusive beaches can enjoy the famous shores of Monte-Carlo, Nice, Antibes, Cannes, Cap Ferrat, Saint-Raphaël and Saint-Tropez, to name only some of the most important, while those who are primarily looking for peace and tranquillity far from the crowds and surrounded by the beauty of nature can take their pick from the hundreds of little bays, picturesque inlets and harbors, some of which are not easily accessible, scattered along the rougher parts of the coast, or along the enchanting swimming areas in the Hyères archipelago - the islands of Porquerolles, Port-Cros, Bagaud and du Levant - wrapped like precious jewels in uncontaminated natural surroundings.

This dual nature of the Côte d'Azur, which is often evident, is a sign of the great richness of the region (and often even of individual towns), which is truly capable of satisfying any desire without losing any of its own character, traditions or beauty. Along the coast, large, famous vacation resorts frequented by thousands of people not only for their beauty, but also for their modern structures, fashionable bars and restaurants, top quality tourist attractions and characteristic worldly tradition coexist with smaller, less famous areas that are in no way outdone by their "big sisters," except, perhaps, in the crowds of tourists, luxurious hotels or high society personalities walking down their streets. The same holds for parts of certain towns. For example, Saint-Tropez, the undisputed queen of worldly tourism on the Côte d'Azur since the 1950's, offers both the spectacle of its port full of exclusive yachts and luxury boats and the town's central square, where life seems to go on as usual, heedless of the noise of the crowds and the fashions of the moment. One aspect which all towns of the region have in common is historical, artistic and cultural richness. It is truly not an exaggeration to say that each individual town on the Côte d'Azur, from the large cities to the small seaside villages, is extremely interesting culturally and offers not only natural beauty, but also first rate art. Town plans which often meld concepts from various epochs provide a background to ancient prehistoric remains, vestiges of Roman times, medieval buildings that reveal Provençal, Ligurian or even Tuscan influence, 16th century castles, splendid baroque monuments, elegant villas, 19th century private residences and public buildings, refined Belle Époque works, surprising architecture from the 1950's, and modern complexes completed over the past few decades which are both greatly admired and harshly criticized. It is an extraordinary mix of natural and historic fascination, tradition and modernity, before which it is impossible to remain indifferent. This is fully evidenced in the numerous works of art which have blessed this region, from medieval times to the dawn of the 20th century, when the Côte d'Azur was discovered by painters, men of letters, musicians and artists in general, to the present, with masterpieces no less superb than the natural setting that surrounds them.

A historic, artistic and vacation center, this town owes its particularly mild climate to the Maritime Alps that flank and protect it. Inhabited since medieval times, as evidenced by the remains found in the nearby grottos of Balzi Rossi (in Italy) and Vallonnet, Menton first belonged to the Genoese. In the 13th century it fell under the control of the French, who fought the Grimaldis of Monaco for it almost until the end of the Second World War. The modern part of the city, extremely popular with the aristocracy as early as the Belle Époque, offers splendid walks along the sea and two beautiful sandy beaches overlooked by the luxuriant green of botanical gardens - the exotic garden of Val Rahmeh at Garavan, the Parc des Colombières on Avenue Bac and the Parc Pian. From the old port a stairway ascends to the upper part of the old city, where the magnificent baroque church of Saint-Michel stands on a lovely gray and white church square that bears the Grimaldi coat of arms. Built in 1675 but with a facade that dates to more recent times (1819), this church

1) View of Menton, with the church of St.
   Michel in the background
2) Church of St. Michel
3-4) Characteristic glimpses of the city

4

is famous for its interior decorated with precious works of art, including the 17th century Adoration of the Shepherds by Orazio Ferrari. The old heart of Menton grew up around the church of Saint-Michel and is known for the fascinating medieval appearance of its narrow streets and little squares and the architecture of many of its buildings, flanked by other baroque monuments such as the Chapelle de la Conception and the Chapelle de la Miséricorde. In summer Menton hosts the Chamber Music Festival and also is the home of various important museums, including the extremely comprehensive Regional Prehistory Museum, the museum dedicated to the contemporary artist Jean Cocteau, and, in the Parc de la Madone, the Musée Municipal, with important collections of ancient and modern art.

1-3) Lemon festival
2) The Biovès garden
4) Nighttime view
5) The Palace of Europe
6) The Casino

5

6

ROQUEBRUNE

This lovely medieval town grew up on the rocky slopes of a hill, around the castle of the House of Grimaldi, which retained control over both it and Menton until 1860. Built in the 10th century for defensive purposes, the building was transformed into a castle during the Renaissance. The last floor of the structure, which includes two old towers (from the 10th and 12th centuries), served as the residence of the lord of the castle. It now holds a museum which displays the original furnishings in various rooms. The present-day baroque structure of the church of Sainte-Marguerite, dating back to the 17th century, hides the Romanesque origins of the building, with beautiful paintings and colorful stuccos inside. A faint trace of 1st century Rome remains at Cap-Martin, the modern area of Roquebrune that extends along the promontory to the foot of the village. The famous architect Le Corbusier often stayed here, where his "cabanon" can now be admired.

Views of the old city standing sheltered on the flanks of the cliffs.

ROQUEBRUNE

1) The beach with Menton in the back ground
2) Le Pirate (The Pirate)
3) Cap Martin
4) Cap Martin - general view
5) The beach

2

3

1

Surrounded by an aura of glamour, the principality is located on the stretch of the Côte d'Azur between Cap d'Ail and Cap Martin. A sovereign and independent state in the form of a constitutional hereditary monarchy, its economy is primarily based on trade, business and tourism. Only a part of its population is Monacan of Italian origin, while over half of its residents are French, Italian or other nationalities, often those attracted by the idea of a fiscal paradise (its residents do not pay taxes). In the 6th century B.C. the Greeks of Focea established a port on the site of the present-day principality of Monaco, where many traces of human settlements have been found dating back to prehistoric times. This port served as a landing for the commercial maritime traffic of the Phoenicians, Carthaginians, Romans and Saracens, who established a colony here in the 10th century. In the 12th century the Genoese took over the area, which was then overwhelmed by the conflict between the Guelphs and the Ghibellines that bloodied Italy during this period. The year 1297 signaled the rise to power of the House of Grimaldi, which still reigns through Prince Rainier; dressed as a monk, Francesco Grimaldi, who had been exiled from Genoa, and several faithful followers succeeded in occupying the castle (built early in that century). Subsequent events nevertheless did not go well for

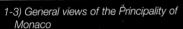

1-3) General views of the Principality of Monaco
4) A scene from the Formula One Grand Prix of Monte-Carlo

2

1

him, and the Grimaldis did not take permanent control of Monaco until 1308. In 1489 France recognized its independence. From 1524 to 1651 Fort Hercule, as today's principality was called at that time, based on a tradition that Hercules had founded the ancient port, was a protectorate of the crown of Spain. During this period (1612) the title of lords of Grimaldi was conferred. In 1641 a peace treaty was signed with France that ensured French control of the principality until 1814, when it returned once again to the House of Grimaldi. After a brief period in which it became a protectorate of Sardinia (1815), Monaco once again enjoyed French protection and in 1865 was united with France through a customs union treaty. The city is divided into four distinct districts: Monaco-Ville, the oldest part of the city, nestled on a rocky promontory by the sea, La Condamine, a modern residential and business center at the foot of the fortress, Monte-Carlo, the luxurious and renowned district of skyscrapers,

1) Monaco - the cathedral
2 - 3) Glimpses of the city
4) The stadium
5) Prince Albert I
6) The fortress of Monaco seen from the Exotic Garden
7) Panoramic view and the beach

the Casino and the most prestigious hotels, and Fontvieille, where the splendid Jardin Exotique is located. Monaco-Ville, the governmental seat, is situated on a rocky terrace 60 meters above sea level. In the old city, traversed by picturesque streets characteristic of the medieval urban plan, is the grandiose royal Palace, constructed over various periods on the site of the earlier castle built by the Genoese in 1215. Located on the most panoramic point of the fortress, it has elegant, opulent interiors (some of which can be visited) decorated by precious works of art, and its south wing (dating back to the 15th century) holds the interesting Musée Napoléonien et des Archives de Palais. Near the palace is the cathedral of Monaco (1875), where the remains of former princes are buried (for a description of the Musée Océanographique, see below). Overlooking the port at the foot of Monaco-Ville is the Condamine district, where the

1) The serene and dignified Palace of Monaco, the residence of Their Serene Highnesses
2) The Clock Tower
3) The monumental gate of the Palace
4) View of the court of honor and the stairway that leads to the Hercules Gallery
5) The Napoleonic Museum
6) The Blue Hall
7) The York Room
8) Pendulum (18th century) - Louis XV room

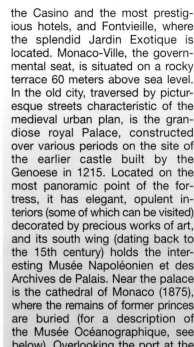

8

church consecrated to Saint-Dévote, patron saint of the principality, is located. The building was constructed in 1860 on the site of an earlier chapel built in the 11th century on the place where, according to tradition, the remains of the saint, martyred in the 3rd century, arrived by ship. Another popular tourist port is located opposite the Fontvieille zone, a residential area adorned not only by the Jardin Exotique (see below), but also by a large park including the famous Princess Grace rose gardens, where over one hundred varieties of roses grow. Behind the park is the extremely modern Louis II athletic complex. The Monte-Carlo district, synonymous with luxurious edifices, exclusive boutiques, wealth, worldliness and sports, is above all famous for its Casino (see below), but also contains other curiosities, such as the beautiful Musée des Poupées Automates, with one of the largest collections of mechanical dolls in the world.

1) Portrait of Princess Grace with Prince Albert and Princess Caroline
2) The Guard Room
3) The Hall of Mirrors
4) The Throne Room

5

Located in a magnificent white stone building built onto the fortress in a panoramic position directly overlooking the sea, the Musée Océanographique was built by order of Prince Albert I of Monaco, a great enthusiast of the marine sciences who opened the museum in 1910. The institution, the most important of the principality, includes not only the museum, but also a prestigious research laboratory entirely dedicated to oceanography. The extremely comprehensive museum aquarium, which includes fully ninety sea water tanks, is populated by marine animal and plant species from all the oceans on the planet, housed in environments that perfectly recreate their various natural habitats. The zoological oceanography room on the ground floor features displays of skeletons of various marine mammals (including sea unicorns, killer whales and a whale twenty meters long which was personally captured by Albert I) and examples of numerous more or less rare marine species, which are also on display in the rooms on the upper floor. The museum also offers a broad panorama of the technology of oceanographic exploration, including models of boats, ships and scientific instruments utilized in underwater research. Splendid documentaries filmed by Jacques Cousteau are shown in the large popular science hall.

6

7

1) The Oceanography Museum
2) Paracanthurus Hepatus; blue and yellow surgeonfish
3) Gaterin orientalis
4) Balistes vetula
5) The whale room
6) Mosaic with marine animal motifs
7) Marble statue depicting Prince Albert on the bridge of his ship
8) General view of the Aquarium
9) Chaetodon Octofasciatus

8

9

EXOTIC GARDEN (JARDIN EXOTIQUE)

Located on the northwest slopes of the principality, the Exotic Garden (Jardin Exotique) stretches out on a rocky cliff facing the sea, with an excellent view and a perfect climate, which is particularly mild and suitable for the cultivation of exotic plant species. The various terraces that comprise it, connected to each other by paths and walkways that offer splendid views of the principality and the sea, constitute an ideal habitat for almost seven thousand varieties of cacti and other succulents, some of which are quite rare. Numerous plants with strange and sometimes spectacular shapes and brightly colored flowers were imported from the semi-arid areas of Mexico and Africa and have found conditions here ideal for luxuriant growth and reproduction. The so-called Grotte de l'Observatoire, a natural grotto which descends 60 meters underground, is also located in the garden. In its first room, traces of human habitation have been found dating back to prehistoric times. The remains discovered are on display in the nearby Prehistoric Anthropology Museum. The other rooms of the cave can also be visited and are decorated with strangely shaped stalactites and stalagmites.

1) Consolea Rubescens; Antilles cactus
2) Parodia Scopaoides
3) Fenestraria Aurantiaca
4) Lampranthus Coccineus

Accessible from the Jardin Exotique, this quite comprehensive and attractive museum is entirely dedicated to prehistoric human settlements in the area between the grottos of Balzi Rossi and Vallonet and the city of Nice. In addition to the collection of skeletons of Homo sapiens, including examples of Cro-Magnon, Neanderthal and Grimaldi Negroid man, there are tombs, animal fossils and various types of tools on display, including primitive utensils and decorative stone necklaces. Numerous display cases show human bones belonging to hominids of various prehistoric eras, while one room displays remains from various periods ranging from Neolithic to Roman times. Of particular interest is the collection of animal bones found on the Côte d'Azur, including remains of animals such as woolly mammoths, reindeer, hippopotami and elephants, all of which evidently populated the region in the distant past.

1) Great Hall
2) Cave - bear

2

THE CASINO

In 1848 Monaco enjoyed a privileged position: under the protection of France, the principality was able to prosper and enjoy a period of relative tranquillity. But in that year an unexpected event occurred that paradoxically signaled the beginning of a totally unanticipated economic fortune. Menton and Roquebrune, the nearby towns acquired by the principality as early as the 14th century (in 1346 and 1355 respectively), which for some time had been chafing at their lack of independence, rebelled against the Monacan lords and officially demanded to be separated from Monaco. For the principality, which received enormous annual financial revenues from both towns, this spelled a grave loss (Menton and Roquebrune were later sold to Napoleon III in 1861) which severely threatened its wealth. Not seeing any other solutions capable of obviating this situation, and in order to ensure continued large revenues for the coffers of the principality, in 1856 the prince of Monaco decided to open a casino for tourists. At first the casino was located right in Monaco, but its immediate success

1-2) Views of the Monte Carlo-Casino
3-4) View and detail of the Hall of Europe
5) The fabulous main card room of the Casino

made it quite evident that the building that housed it was too small and modest to meet the needs of habitual and potential users. In 1862 the casino was transferred to the Monte Carlo area, which at that time did not enjoy its present-day fame and prestige, but which was nevertheless an area where new structures could be built. The structure built to house the casino once again proved to be inadequate, for reasons which included the fact that it was located in an area which was essentially isolated and lacking in services. The present-day Casino was not constructed until 1878, the year in which the architect Charles Garnier built this monumental edifice overlooking the sea. Times have changed, and, due primarily to the frenetic activity and enormous capital of François Blanc (a casino director who obtained the license for the local casino), Monte-Carlo has transformed into a lively city where an entire district of luxury buildings has grown up around the Casino, which is now the destination of wealthy vacationers willing

1) Detail of the Royal Box
2) The Cabaret
3) General view of the Opera Theater

3

to tempt fortune with dizzying sums of money that provide fully 60% of the total revenues of the principality. Garnier (who also built the Opéra in Paris), designed the Casino as a true temple of luxury and splendor, which can be seen even from the elegant facade crowned with large cupolas flanked by four small side towers. With its precious marbles and the twenty-eight onyx Ionic columns that adorn them, the large lobby leads into the two main sections of the building. The first, right across from the entrance, is occupied by the magnificent Opéra hall (Salle Garnier), which offers a frame of gold, sculpted decorations and frescoes for various types of art shows (from concerts to theater). The rest of the palace is occupied by various gambling rooms (the entrance is to the left of the main lobby), adorned by sumptuous, stylish furnishings and splendid paintings. In the Salle Ganne, the vast hall on the lower floor reached by descending an extremely elegant staircase, is the refined Casino nightclub. In the front of the building, embellished by splendid flowerbeds, is the spectacular Des Spélugues complex with the prestigious Monte-Carlo Convention Center and the Auditorium, designed by the architect Vasarely.

1) The exterior of the Hotel de Paris as seen from the Casino
2) The hall of the Hotel de Paris
3) Garnier Palace and several dolls on the stairway

LA TURBIE

Located on one of the most scenic points of the Grand Corniche, right above Monte Carlo, the city owes its fame to the Alps Monument that was erected on the top of the hill between 7-6 B.C. La Turbie stands on the traces of the ancient Via Julia Augusta, the road that connected cisalpine and transalpine Gaul and which still today crosses the city and leads up to the Monument. The remains of this grandiose monument offer only a glimpse of what its original glory must have been, 40 meters and two stories high and crowned by a cupola with a statue of Augustus. The structure was built at the point that marked the boundary between the two Gauls, to celebrate the victory of Rome over all Alpine peoples (16-14 B.C.).

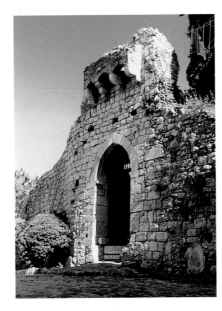

Overall view of La Turbie with details of the old road; the Alps Monument built in honor of the Emperor Augustus and stele dedicated to Napoleon Bonaparte.

2 AVRIL 1796
NAPOLEON BONAPARTE
A LA TETE DE L'ARMEE D'ITALIE
EN ROUTE
VERS SON P.C. D'ALBENGA
EST L'HOTE EN CETTE DEMEURE
DU CHEVALIER MICHEL ROSSETTI
MAIRE CI-DEVANT BAYLE ·
SON ARRIERE GARDE
ICI AU CANTONNEMENT
BONAPARTE
GAGNE MENTON POUR LA NUIT

ROTARY CLUB LOCI POSUIT
2-4-71

The town is divided into two quite distinct parts: Èze Village, located on a rocky slope facing the sea in an exceptionally scenic position, and Èze-Bord-de-Mer, a modern swimming resort protected by rocky cliffs.

The territory of Èze was originally occupied by a Ligurian settlement situated at the foot of the present-day town, and was subsequently conquered by Phoenicians, Romans and Turks. The 12th century signaled the beginning of the signory of Èze and the shift of the inhabited area up onto the slope. As can immediately be seen upon entering the town through the 14th century fortified gate, Èze-Village retains a lovely medieval town structure, with steep, narrow streets often connected by steps, as well as the medieval architecture of its stone houses and monuments, such as the beautiful 14th century Chapelle des Pénitents Blancs, never showy but always full of charm. On the top of the hill, with the ruins of the old 14th century castle, is a splendid exotic garden.

Situated in a position overlooking the Mediterranean, Èze still has a typically medieval appearance

This town, facing the sea and protected by the gently rolling hills, is one of the most seductive swimming resorts on the Côte d'Azur, and is particularly appreciated for its very mild climate. The most beautiful part of the town is located around the green Petite Afrique quarter and Boulevard Alsace-Lorraine.

Following the boulevard, you will reach the splendid Bay des Fourmis, at the tip of which is the most famous monument of Beaulieu, Villa Kérylos. The structure, built by the archeologist Théodore Reinach, was constructed in 1928 as a reproduction of the most luxurious palaces of ancient Greece. The precious construction materials (marble from Carrara, high quality woods and alabaster) provide a backdrop to frescoes that reproduce ancient originals, furniture copied from decorations on ancient vases, mosaics, amphorae, small statues and other original items from ancient times. Around the villa is a splendid park overlooking the sea.

1-5) Its position at the foot of a rocky slope covered with olive groves makes it a popular area year round. Its port is magnificent.
2) The Beaulieu Casino
3) Santa Maria de Olivo
4) Fourmis harbor and Villa Kérylos
6) General view

1

5

6

VILLEFRANCHE-SUR-MER

After leaving Beaulieu-sur-Mer and visiting the marvelous Ile-de-France villa of the Fondation Musée Ephrussi (1905-1912) at Cap Ferrat, with its precious collections of art and its splendid garden, continue toward the bay of Villefranche, opposite the Bay des Fourmis. The town, overlooking a deep, quite beautiful harbor protected by green hills, maintains a special charm, with its old port, citadel and the picturesque little streets that run through the 17th century historic center. Villefranche was founded in the 14th century by Charles of Anjou, and at the end of the century was ceded to the Savoys, who made it into a major fortified port. The House of Savoy built the citadel, now the site of important museums, in the second half of the 16th century. The baroque church of Saint-Michel should also be visited, along with the Chapelle de Saint-Pierre, with its interior decorated by Jean Cocteau.

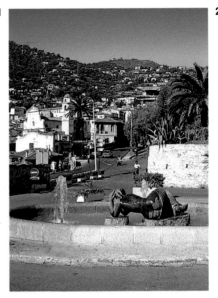

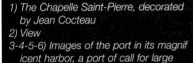

1) The Chapelle Saint-Pierre, decorated by Jean Cocteau
2) View
3-4-5-6) Images of the port in its magnif icent harbor, a port of call for large steamers and war ships.

The city, famous for its Carnival, its festival of flowers and its artistic monuments, as well as for the beauty of its location and its climate, is located in an area which was already inhabited by humans over 400,000 years ago.

Around the 4th century B.C. the Greek colonists of Focea occupied the site, which they called Nikaia, and were later succeeded by peoples of Ligurian origin.

Two centuries later the Romans arrived and founded a town (Cemenelum) on the hill of Cimiez, which quickly became the most important military and administrative center in the region, overwhelming the Greek Nikaia.

It was not until the 10th century, after the end of the nightmare of barbarian and Saracen devastation that had caused irreparable damage to Cemenelum in particular, did Nice, an episcopal seat since the 5th century, reassume a preeminent position, placing itself under the protection of the Count of Provence.

But the city's desire for independence, which had manifested as

1) General view of the city
2) Elysée Palace Hotel
3) The Massena Museum seen from the outside
4) Rühl Casino

2

1

early as the 12th century, inspired it to abandon the Provençal dynasty in 1388 and to voluntarily place itself under the control of Count Amadeus VII of Savoy. Nice remained tied to the House of Savoy almost until 1860, with shifting fortunes.

The abrupt disownment had its consequences, and during the 16th century was city was assaulted time and time again by French and Turkish troops, although each time it managed to withstand the attacks.

Having overcome these assaults, the fortress of Nice (fortified in the 16th century) was nevertheless razed to the ground by the French in 1706.

Favored by Napoleon, who stayed here for long periods after 1792, the year in which the city requested to be annexed to France, Nice (where Giuseppe Garibaldi was born in 1807) returned to the Savoys in 1814, and only the referendum of 1860 sanctioned its permanent transfer to France.

From this time on the "queen of the Riviera," frequented primarily by the English since the late 18th century, experienced a surprising

1) A modern fountain
2-4) The garden of the Esplanade du Paillon
3) Panoramic view of the Albert I gardens

3

4

1

2

spate of development, both in economic terms and with the construction of large hotels, elegant villas and luxurious buildings.

The "golden age" of tourism in Nice had begun, and continues to this day. If a visit to Nice must of necessity include a walk along the splendid Promenade des Anglais, the museums and monuments of this city of a thousand surprises are also a must.

Those who prefer a cultural visit can choose between the Musée Terra Amata, the Musée Masséna, dedicated to the history and art of the city, the Musée des Beaux-Arts, with its antique and contemporary collections, the Musée d'Art Naïf, the Musée Naval, the Musée d'Art Moderne et Contemporain, the Musée d'Histoire Naturelle, or, at Cimiez, the prestigious Marc Chagall and Matisse museums and the lavish Musée d'Archéologie.

Art and architecture soar to their greatest heights in the city, both in the streets and the beautiful squares crowned by buildings, and in the monuments, for example the church of Saints Martin and Augustin, the oldest parish in Nice (16th century), the baroque cathedral of Sainte-Réparate, and the 17th century churches of Saint-Jacques and Saint-Guillaume. Baroque style triumphs in the luxurious Lascaris palace with its elegant monumental staircase, in the refined chapels of the Pénitents Blancs and the Pénitents Noirs, and in the marvelous Chapelle de l'Annonciation. The old Franciscan monastery (15th-17th centuries) erected on the hill of Cimiez, with its splendid Gothic church of Notre-Dame-de-l'Assomption, are the sites of greatest interest in this part of the city, along with the remains of Roman times (thermal baths from the 3rd century B.C., amphithea-

3

4

5

1) The Chapelle de la Miséricorde
2-4) Typical street of the city
3) The flower market
5) Potter's sign
6) Russian-Orthodot Cathedral

6

ters, an early Christian baptistry, parts of the original oppidum and several necropolises).

1) The Acropolis
2-3) Museum of Modern and Contemporary Art
4) General view of the Apollon Auditorium

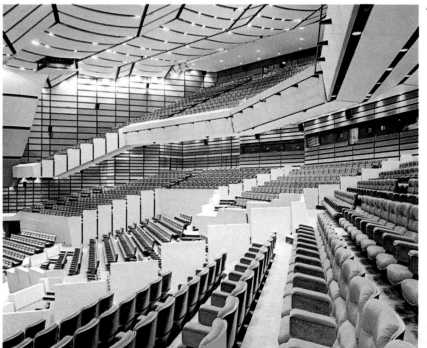

Views of Carnival and the battle of flowers

THE CASTLE

Nothing remains of the original castle of Nice that stood on the hill overlooking the sea and was destroyed in 1706. The site, served by an elevator, is nevertheless one of the most spectacular panoramic points overlooking the city and the Bay des Anges, and also contains interesting ruins of the old medieval cathedral near the 19th century Bellanda tower (where the Musée Naval is located).

1) The artificial waterfall
2) The unique little train that carries tourists to the Castle
3) The ruins inside the Castle: the rocks of ancient Nikaia

2

3

1

Until the mid-18th century Nice did not have a true port, but only a docking area located at the foot of the fortress, frequented by fishing and trading vessels.

Charles Emanuele III of Savoy ordered the construction of a port, which was then expanded and improved between the early 20th century and 1970, through the construction of an outer harbor. The ancient port of Lympia, which had already been utilized by the Greeks of Nikaia and the Romans of Cemenelum, now accommodates ferries sailing to Corsica.

Boats of all types, from commercial craft to sailboats, yachts and little fishing boats, daily crowd the more modern portion of the port, which is always bustling.

Nearby are the grotto of Lazaret and the Terra Amata area, precious testimony to human presence in the area even in prehistoric times.

Views of the port of Lympia

CAGNES-SUR-MER

Founded in the early 14th century, the town, surrounded by beautiful flowering hills, is only a short distance from Nice. It consists of three districts: the first and innermost area, Haut-de-Cagnes, still conserves some of its medieval character; the second, Cros-de-Cagnes, is the swimming resort; and the third, Cagnes-Ville, is the modern area and is located halfway between the first two. The town is also famous for its racetrack, where important international races take place. The most beautiful and interesting town center is Haut-de-Cagnes, the 14th century town dominated by the old castle and still closed within its original medieval walls. The old city offers splendid views along its picturesque, often twisting lanes and in its squares lined with old buildings, some of which date back to the 14th century. Its most important monuments include the church of Saint-Pierre, which features a baroque nave and a small Gothic aisle that contains the tombs of the Grimaldis of Cagnes, and the Chapelle de Notre-Dame-de-Protection, adorned with beautiful 16th century frescoes. In the upper part of the town, the elegant inner rooms (in various architectural styles, from medieval to 17th century) of the 14th century castle house an interesting art museum that displays various collections of paintings. One section is dedicated to olive growing, which is quite common on the hills of the area. The Festival Room on the second floor is decorated by a large trompe-l'oeil from 1624. An international festival of contemporary painting is held each year at the castle. A short distance outside the town is the Musée Renoir, set up in the house where the great painter lived the last years of his life. It holds objects that belonged to the artist and some of his beautiful autograph works.

1) Port St. Laurent: port Saint Laurent and Atoll Beach
2-5-6-7-8) Cagnes-sur-Mer: includes the old city with its interlocking houses and the Grimaldi Castle
3-4) Cros-de-Cagnes: a small fishing port and swimming resort. Famous for its race track.

MARINA BAIE DES ANGES

Located on the enchanting Bay des Anges, this exclusive swimming resort is famous in particular for its modern, controversial residential complex designed by the architect André Minangoy. Standing immediately behind the beach and the tourist port, it includes four gigantic white buildings shaped like strange rounded pyramids, each one twenty floors high and divided into luxurious apartments with a view of the bay. At the base of the pyramids are elegant shops and cafés. The horizontal lines of the terraces gradually sloping upward and the bright flowers that decorate them during the summer do not fully succeed in lightening the heaviness of the buildings. This is both one of the most criticized and most praised architectural works on the Côte d'Azur, and is recognized equally for its boldness and originality as well as for its dubious impact on the environment in an area known for its enchanting scenery and natural beauty. Marina Baie des Anges is administratively a part of the nearby city of Villeneuve-Loubet, located inland a short distance from the sea. Of medieval origins, the gracious town is dominated by the castle of the lords of Villeneuve, built in the 12th century and later remodeled. The imposing pentagonal tower that stands on the castle is even older, probably dating from the 9th century. The castle is distinguished by two rings of walls that surround it. The higher walls are the oldest, while the lower walls date from the 16th century. Apart from its antique charm, Villeneuve-Loubet is famous for its curious Musée de l'Art Culinaire. Entirely dedicated to haute cuisine and gourmets, the museum is located in the birthplace of the famous chef August Escoffier (1846-1935), the inventor of the delicious peach Melba.

1) Scenic view
2-3) Two aspects of Marina Baie des Anges

Immersed in a landscape of splendid hills cultivated with vineyards and olive groves with the buttresses of the Maritime Alps in the background, in the past this was a fortified town famous for its impregnability. Today it is one of the most well-known and popular artistic communities of France.

Prosperous during the Middle Ages, it was fortified with imposing bastions in the early 15th century, and again in the mid-16th century, with walls designed by the architects Mandon and Vauban that are still visible today. Despite the construction of these walls, which required the demolition of hundreds of houses, Saint-Paul was unable to withstand the assaults of first the Savoys and then the Hungarians, who occupied it at the beginning of the 18th century. By the next century, the center had begun to lose much of its importance and was left behind by the neighboring towns of Vence and Cagnes. Having become a tranquil agricultural village, during the 1920's it began to attract numerous personalities from the art world (from Modigliani to Bonnard), who were then followed by great and celebrated painters, sculptors, poets and men of letters, including contemporary artists, who contributed to making it an artists' community of prime importance. Right outside the walls, the prestigious Auberge de la Colombe d'Or is testimony to its role as a favorite gathering place for artists, with its marvelous collections of art that include works by Braque, Matisse and Utrillo. A visit to the town itself can follow a pleasant walk along the 16th century communications trench of the walls (open the whole way). The panorama from the northern gate to the southern gate, of Vence and Nice respectively, is superb, with enchanting views both seaward to Cap d'Antibes and inland, with the peaks of the Alps and the Esterel range in the distance. In the interior, along Rue Grande, which runs down the middle of

1) General view of Saint-Paul
2) The Great Fountain

Saint-Paul, are beautiful 16th and 17th century buildings, mostly occupied by artisan workshops, art shops and elegant crafts boutiques. In the cozy central square is a lovely old urn fountain with a wash basin. Right in front of the tall tower that houses the city hall, the church of Saint-Paul, originally from the 12-13th centuries but remodeled in the 15th and 18th centuries, preserves a precious Treasury and valuable paintings within its baroque interior.

The Fondation Maeght, located on a hill near Saint-Paul, dedicates its various activities exclusively to art, and organizes shows and conventions on the theme. It is located in an original modern building with splendid architecture that includes elements created by great artists such as Chagall, Miró, Braque and others, numerous works by whom appear in the foundation's extensive permanent collection, along with other works by some of the most famous modern and contemporary artists.

1) The bastions
2) Miró maze
3) Characteristic glimpse
4) Giacometti Courtyard
5) Tilio Fountain

VENCE

Dominated by rocky buttresses and immersed in the hills planted with vineyards and olive groves that extend from Nice to Cannes, this splendid medieval town is one of the most beautiful cities in the immediate inland area. The old city, with its alleyways, squares and picturesque little streets, is surrounded by the original, elliptical-shaped medieval walls with their three beautiful gates. Full of artistic beauties, Vence truly became a city of art and culture after the 1950's, when numerous artists began to frequent it and Saint-Paul. For example, Matisse designed the Chapelle du Rosaire and its marvelous interior decorations, and Chagall created the beautiful mosaic in the cathedral, which in its turn is a mosaic of various architectural styles from the 11th to the 19th centuries.

1) *Peyra Fountain*
2) *General view of Vence*
3) *Picturesque old street in the city center*
4) *Place Frêne*
5) *Chapelle des Pénitents Blancs (1614)*

GOURDON

Perched at the tip of a rocky spur in an exceptionally panoramic position (which is especially enchanting from the church square), this town preserves beautiful old houses, most of which are occupied by boutiques and artisan workshops, and is dominated by the massive 13th century castle. Distinguished by its Moorish-style architectural details, the structure contains an interesting historical museum and a museum of naïf art.

1) The picturesque village at the top of the mountain
2) Wolf Gorges

1

2

Surrounded by hills, this town, which was already flourishing in the 10th century, united with Pisa and Genoa in the 12th century and gained its autonomy, which it lost in 1227 when it was subjected to the Duke of Provence. From that moment on its fortunes shifted, and the town was in fact destroyed in the 16th and 18th centuries. The birthplace of the great painter Jean-Honoré Fragonard (1732-1806), until the 17th century Grasse boasted a prestigious perfumery tradition, the history of which is preserved in the International Museum of Perfumery. The old city still looks like a typical medieval Provençal town, with its picturesque streets and squares and the medieval architecture of its houses (especially Place aux Aires) and monuments, including the cathedral, of Romanesque origins, the bishopric (today the city hall) and the Clock Tower, both of which latter date from the 13th century. Grasse is also a lively cultural center, and in addition to the perfumery museum also contains other important museums (The Provence Art and History Museum, the Fragonard Museum and the Navy Museum).

1-2) Views
3) The Convention Center by night
4) Place Aires and the flower market

A famous and popular tourist resort, Antibes is located halfway between Nice and Cannes. The Greeks of Focea founded it in the 4th century B.C., on land formerly inhabited by peoples of Etruscan and Ligurian origins, and named it Antipolis. A flourishing trading center, the town became quite important in Roman times, culminating in its being named as an episcopal seat in 442. Plundered by barbarians and Saracens in the Middle Ages, when all traces of its Roman era history were destroyed, it fell into the hands of the Grimaldis in the late 14th century and then passed to the French. Henry IV took advantage of its strategic position and built mighty fortified structures here. The walls, which were later expanded and strengthened by the famous architect Vauban, were almost completely demolished in the late 19th century. A visit to the old city could begin with a walk along the sea down Avenue Admiral-de-Grasse. This scenic road follows the only stretch of the original bastions which survived the demolition of 1895. Following the picturesque inner streets, often connected by stairs, you will come to the church of the Immaculate Conception with its baroque facade and Romanesque apse and transept that date back to the years of its original construction (12th-13th centuries). The bell tower, which is a guard tower dating from the 13th century, is also medieval. The square tower, the patrol walk and a few other elements from the Grimaldi castle, built on the site of the ancient Greek acropolis and remodeled in the 16th century, date back to the 12th century. With its chapel decorated by a lovely Deposition by Antonio Aundi (1539), the building is the site of the prestigious Musée Picasso, which displays numerous works done by the artist during his stay on the Côte d'Azur. Other interesting museums are located in the four ancient bastions of the town.

1) Images of the bastion and the castle
2) General view of Antibes and its harbor
3-4) Characteristic glimpses
5) The castle and a glimpse of the port
6) A corner of the city

6

Of relatively recent origins (it was founded in the last twenty years of the 19th century), Juan-les-Pins is one of the most popular and luxurious towns on the Côte d'Azur.

It is located in a splendid position right at the end of Golfe-Juan, halfway between the emerald green, exclusive promontory of Cap-d'Antibes and the tip of Croisette and connected to Cannes by the renowned boulevard of the same name.

A long white sand beach runs along the town's stretch of coast, which is part of the municipality of Antibes, next to the luxuriant pine forest that is one of Juan-les-Pins' natural beauties. Since the mid-1950's, the town has attracted tourists primarily interested not only in the beauty of its location, but also in the worldly pleasures and nightlife offered by the numerous trendy locales and the casino.

The town also hosts quite important cultural shows and events, such as the prestigious International Jazz Festival.

1) Panoramic view
2) The Garden Beach Hotel
3) Glimpse of the seaside promenade

2

VALLAURIS

In the Middle Ages this town nestled among the hills belonged to the monks of Lérins, who in 1227 built a castle and founded a convent here, which was destroyed in the late 14th century along with the town. Vallauris remained abandoned until 1500, when Ligurian families once again populated it and devoted themselves to the production of ceramics. This activity, which was already flourishing in the area at the time of Tiberius, received new creative inspiration in 1947 when Pablo Picasso came to live in the town for a period of time, and is now the pride of Vallauris. The monks' castle, destroyed in 1568, was restored and now is the site of the Musée Municipal, which displays artistic ceramics (including those by Picasso) and an important collection of paintings by the Florentine artist Alberto Magnelli. The Musée Pablo Picasso is located in the splendid Romanesque chapel of the former medieval monastery, decorated by Picasso's large mural, War and Peace. The artist also created the bronze statue Man with Ram in Place Isnard (with the beautiful church of Saint-Martin).

1) Picasso Museum
2) Oil mill (18th century)
3) Production of dishes
4) Glimpse of the city center
5) Old Mill dishes

Vallauris and the coastal town form a single municipality. Due to its good position, overlooking a small bay sheltered by the flowering hills of Vallauris and the islands of Lérins to the other side, it has become a renowned tourist and beach resort. Numerous vacationers come here every year, attracted by the beautiful beach, the tourist harbor with its crowds of lovely sailing vessels and off-board motorboats, and the picturesque surrounding towns.

Apart from its natural and scenic beauty, Golfe-Juan owes its notoriety primarily to a historical event: it was here, in fact, that on March 1, 1815, Napoleon, returning from the island of Elba, disembarked with his small fleet and retinue of one thousand men. A mosaic was created on the quay of the port in order to commemorate the event.

A scenic road, Route Napoléon, runs from the town and, crossing the hills of Cannes, continues for about 50 kilometers, offering enchanting views of the bay of Golfe-Juan and the coast.

General views of the city with the beach and port

A movie city par excellence, Cannes is one of the most famous and lively tourist resorts on the Côte d'Azur. Thousands of visitors come here every year, attracted by the mild climate even in the winter, the natural beauty that surrounds it, with the splendid flowering hills inland and the crystal clear sea of the Gulf of Napoule, by its elegant 19th century buildings, and last but not least, by its annual film festival. With ties to the monks on the nearby island of Lerino (Saint-Honorat) that date back to 410, the year the monastery was founded, the town first grew up on the hill of Suquet, where in ancient times first the Greeks and then the Romans settled. In 1788 it obtained its independence from the monastery, but it remained a secondary city for another fifty years or so. In fact, Cannes' golden period did not begin until the first half of the 19th century, signaled by the arrival first of Lord Brougham and then by other wealthy foreigners. Charmed by the beauty of the location, they decided to build on the site (including tourist facilities), and constructed villas and residences with el-

1) General view of Cannes
2-4) The Carlton Hotel
3) The new Festival Palace
5) Majestic Hotel

egant Belle Époque architecture. The most well-known area of Cannes is Boulevard de la Croisette, so called because it runs to the point of the same name that ends east of the Gulf of Napoule. Right at the beginning of the scenic seaside walkway, dotted with exclusive hotels and shops, is the Film Palace (1984), the site of the annual Festival, while at the opposite end, before the Pierre Canto tourist port (one of three in Cannes), the boulevard is bounded by a large park entirely planted with roses (Roseraie). The elegant central districts can be discovered by walking along the beautiful streets behind the Film Palace, while if you walk up the hill of Suquet you will discover Cannes' past in a visit to the remains of the medieval castle (now the home of the Musée de la Castre, with its beautiful archeological and ethnographic collections) and the 16th century church of Notre-Dame-de-l'Espérance.

1-5) Views of the new Festival Palace
2) Fountain with statue near the Festival Palace
3) The casino
4) Panoramic view of Cannes

1

A pleasant beach resort, La Napoule is located just a few kilometers from Cannes on the first slopes of the Esterel range, which extends west from here up to Saint-Raphaël. With its large tourist port, the principal attraction of the town is its beautiful sandy beaches overlooked by a picturesque neo-Gothic castle in the background. Built on the site of a pre-existing 14th century fortress, the building, which includes two square towers from the older structure, was rebuilt and almost completely remodeled by the American sculptor Henry Clews starting in 1918. With his preference for Oriental style and form, the artist transformed the castle into his own private residence and embellished it with numerous works he himself had created, which can still be seen in the museum named after Clews located in the castle.

A short way inland from La Napoule is Mandelieu, famous for its ruins of a pre-1200 chapel and its extensive plantations of fragrant mimosa.

1) The beach and the Castle
2-3) The port and the Agecroft castle

THEOULE-SUR-MER

This elegant seaside town popular for its three beautiful beaches of fine sand, sheltered and protected from the wind, is distinguished by a great castle with battlements and turrets standing on the promenade. In reality, it is an 18th century soap factory which was later restructured and, oddly, transformed into an elegant castle.

1) Panorama
2) View of the Castle

ANTHEOR

A rather small seaside town, Anthéor is a popular swimming resort. The graceful harbor which it overlooks is protected from the rear by a wing of hills dominated by Pic du Cap-Roux. Nearby there is a spectacular view of the brightly colored buttresses of the Esterel range plunging into the waters of the sea.

3) The port
4) The cliffs of red porphyry

This beautiful swimming resort with its two sandy beaches is located along the edges of a deep bay with the Esterel range sheltering it from the back. Here more than anywhere else, the spectacular rocks (which are eruptive and consist primarily of porphyry in various colors, from the predominant red to gray, green, blue and violet) that plunge into the sea take on a splendid red and azure color that, along with the typical vegetation of the Mediterranean scrub, gives this town's landscape a quite special charm. Indeed, the bay of Agay is one of the most enchanting points on this stretch of the Côte d'Azur. It was this characteristic blue porphyry that attracted the Romans (but before them came the Greeks and various Ligurian peoples), who loaded this precious material onto their ships to be used for their most refined construction work. Some milestones and a few remnants of Via Aurelia, which ran not far from the town, are evidence of the ancient Roman settlement, as are the remains discovered on the seabed during underwater archeological excavations, mostly amphorae which were probably part of the cargo of a galley which sank in this part of the sea a few years after the birth of Christ. Like other towns located along the coast in the Corniche de l'Esterel area, Agay was also invaded by Saracen pirates during the early Middle Ages, in attacks which caused sometimes permanent destruction and devastation. The vast beach, dominated by the reddish fan of rocks of Rastel d'Agay, is located next to a smaller, equally sandy coastal area which is much more popular due to its position, which provides some protection from the intense rays of the sun.

1) The beach
2) The port
3) Scenic view

DRAMONT

The beach of this gracious swimming resort, where American troops landed in 1944, is flanked by the great pine forest that extends along the entire cape of Dramont. From the coast a road ascends up to Sémaphore du Dramont, an exceptionally panoramic point that offers spectacular views of the colored rocks (the red ones are marvelous) that drop sheer into the sea, and of the surrounding coast, from the bay of Agay to the gulf of Fréjus.

1) Panorama

BOULOURIS

This seaside town owes its charm to its favorable position and the beautiful beaches that line the sea opposite. Sprinkled with villas surrounded by the green of the nearby pine forest, Boulouris is enchanting due to the spectacular view of Corniche de l'Esterel in the distance, with its rocky offshoots that plunge down to the sea, mixing their characteristic red color with the crystalline azure blue of the water.

2-3) The beach and the port

1

2

3

73

Located a short distance from Fréjus on the gulf of the same name, the particularly mild climate of this charming swimming resort makes it popular with tourists all year round. Behind it the Esterel range rises in the distance, while to the west are the buttresses of the Maures range, plunging down to the sea and forming countless inlets and little bays on a coast stained a lovely red by the porphyry present in the rocks. The beautiful beach, protected by the mountains that crown it, extends to the end of the bay, where there are two large tourist harbors, always crowded with elegant sailing vessels and luxurious off-board motorboats, and the old port where fishing and commercial activities are still concentrated today. Fashionable locales, cafés, restaurants, prestigious hotels and exclusive boutiques are scattered everywhere in this lively tourist town, both on the seaside promenade and in the actual city behind it.

The site of Saint-Raphaël, located at the mouth of the river Argens, was inhabited even in prehistoric times, as evidenced by the megaliths and numerous remains from the period which have been discovered in archeological excavations on the site. Later, the area was settled by peoples of Ligurian origin, who were then supplanted by the Romans who occupied the area in 151 B.C. More interested in nearby Fréjus (which they founded in 49 B.C.) due to its strategic position, the Romans used Saint-Raphaël, which they called Epulias, primarily as a vacation area, as can be seen from the vestiges of a villa from this period equipped with thermal facilities, and a fish hatchery found in the old port area. Roman times were followed by the incursions of Saracen pirates, whose attacks gradually caused the city to be abandoned, with the town turned over to the abbey of Lérins in the 10th century. The monks and then

1) View of the beach
2) Parc St. Lucie
3) The casino

74

3

the Templars, who took over control of the village in the 12th century, improved the luck of Saint-Raphaël, which, having overcome the terrible hardships of malaria and the destruction of war, sank into relative anonymity. In 1799 and again in 1813 the town experienced two important historical events. The first was the landing of Napoleon after his victory in the Egyptian campaign (commemorated by an obelisk in the port), while the second was his departure for the island of Elba after his defeat. But Saint-Raphaël's true golden age did not begin until later, around the mid-19th century, when first the journalist Alphonse Karr and then numerous writers (including Dumas and Maupassant) and artists began to come here, drawn by its enchanting beauty. Personalities from the art world were followed by the social elite of the period, who built splendid holiday residences in the town and turned it into a vacation resort. The old city is located behind the scenic seaside promenades embellished by gardens and elegant eighteenth century architecture, and beyond the railroad tracks that cut through the center of town. It is dominated by the old church of Saint-Pierre, also known as the church of Saint Raphaël or the church of the Templars. It was in fact built by the Templars in the 12th century in Provençal Romanesque style on the site of two earlier buildings, and was then remodeled in the mid-18th century. One chapel holds a curious prehistoric Pagan monolith in red gres.

The presbytery contains the interesting Musée d'Archéologie et Préhistoire, which includes an extensive collection of Roman amphorae found on the seabeds of the coast, dating back to a period between the 5th century B.C. and the 5th century A.D.

2

1) The façade of the church of the Templars
2) The port and the church of the Templars

Nicknamed the "French Pompeii" due to the quantity and importance of the Roman monuments it preserves, the city was founded by Julius Caesar in 49 B.C., who named it Forum Julii.

Within a short time it had become a flourishing center due to its proximity to Via Aurelia and its strategic position, which in 39 B.C. led Augustus to create an important military port on this very site.

The town declined in the Middle Ages and in 940 was destroyed by the Saracens. It was finally rebuilt in 990 at the initiative of bishop Riculfo, who is also responsible for the construction of the cathedral and the new port structures that made it possible for the city to expand its trading activities. In the 17th century the silting up of the port and an epidemic of malaria spelled the end of this new period of well-being.

1) Old portal
2) The beach with Saint Raphael in the background

Photos on pages 78-79: nighttime panorama and the Cathedral

The most significant monument of Forum Julii is the amphitheater. Intended for use by soldiers, it was built in the 2nd century A.D., in part within the shelter of a hill outside the city walls, of which some traces still remain. The ruins of the theater date from the same period, while the 50 kilometer long aqueduct is from the 1st century B.C.

In the area of the Roman port the two fortified citadels can still be seen, Plate-Forme to the east and Butte Saint-Antoine to the west. The Lanterne d'Auguste was built in the Middle Ages on the remains of an earlier Roman lighthouse.

The quite fascinating medieval town of Fréjus is dominated by the episcopal district with its splendid Provençal Gothic-style cathedral, the baptistry from the 5th century and the elegant medieval cloister. The 14th century episcopal palace now serves as the city hall.

The remains of the Arena

COGOLIN

Located slightly inland, this gracious Provençal town (which also includes the nearby sandy beach of Les Marines de Cogolin) extends to the foot of the hills that brush up against the buttresses of the Maures range. Famous for its artisan crafts - carpets, pipes and fishing poles - and for its vineyards, the old city preserves a Romanesque church (11th century) decorated with a precious wood triptych from the 16th century.

Cogolin: panoramic view

SAINT-AYGULF

Covered with very fine sand, the beautiful beach of this gracious swimming resort on the Gulf of Fréjus stands out on a background dominated by rocks that plunge down into the sea and the emerald green forests of pine, oak and eucalyptus that surround the town. Saint-Aygulf offers visitors spectacular views of the gulf coast as well as the majestic buttresses of the Esterel and Maures ranges that rise up in the distance behind it.

Saint-Aygulf: the port

SAINTE-MAXIME

Touristy, worldly and always quite lively, this town directly opposite Saint-Tropez on the west shore of the gulf of the same name features a historic center, dominated by the castle hill, that has remained quite picturesque. The port and the beach, protected by a group of hills, are an irresistible attraction for numerous tourists, who are also drawn by the enchanting view offered by the nearby hill of Sémaphore.

Sainte-Maxime: the beach

Of medieval origins, Grimaud, a populous town not far inland, owes its name to the Grimaldi family, who owned it until the 10th century. Originally founded on the coast and then moved inland to avoid Saracen raiders, the village still preserves the four angular towers of a mighty fortified castle built in the Middle Ages. The picturesque little streets of the town are lined with buildings full of antique charm, including the little Romanesque church of Saint-Michel, and the Chapelle des Pénitents Blancs, which was remodeled in the 15th century.

Overlooking the sea at the end of the gulf of Saint-Tropez is Port-Grimaud, a reinterpretation of a typical seaside town begun in 1966 by the architect François Spoerry. Traversed by canals and equipped with a large port and little sandy beaches nearby, its architectural features preserve old Provençal tradition.

1) Aerial view
2) The old Castle
3) Picturesque corner

An exceptionally famous resort town, Saint-Tropez certainly needs no introduction. The image of its little port brimming with yachts, elegant sailboats and luxurious sailing vessels overlooking the splendid gulf of Saint-Tropez and crowned by the picturesque, pastel-colored houses that surround it, is renowned throughout the world, as are the images of the movie stars and members of high society who, particularly during the 1950's and 1960's but to a great extent even today, have given it life, along with a mass of artists and literary figures enraptured by its beauty and irresistible charm. Yet, until the end of the 19th century, when it was "discovered" by writers and painters, Saint-Tropez was only one of the many gracious seaside towns scattered along the Côte d'Azur, poorly served by a small railway and dedicated primarily to fishing and wine trading. Known to the Greeks and Romans, who built a temple to Hercules here, the town takes its name from San Torpes, a Christian centurion martyred by Nero; a boat bearing the body of the centurion reached the shores of Saint-Tropez, where he was buried and honored in a sanctuary. After centuries of hardship marked by devastating wars and Saracen invasions, at the end of the 14th century the city was abandoned, and only at the end of the following

1) Nighttime view
2) Panoramic view

century was it repopulated by several families of Genoese origin. These families placed themselves under the protection of the seneschal of Provence, who gave Saint-Tropez remarkable autonomy, allowing the town to turn into a sort of little independent republic. In 1637 the fleet of Saint-Tropez gained a spectacular victory over twenty Spanish ships which were trying to take over four French ships. This episode, perhaps the most glorious in local history, is still remembered today in a bravade, a picturesque procession through the streets of the city each year on June 15. Another more famous and popular bravade takes place on May 16-18 and culminates as a wooden bust of the patron of Saint-Tropez is paraded through the city. Apart from the port and its lovely sandy beaches, a visit to Saint-Tropez holds interesting surprises for tourists, including the picturesque streets that wind behind the port, enlivened by numerous fashionable locales, art galleries, elegant boutiques and curious shops. The Musée de l'Annonciade, located in a 17th century chapel, displays precious paintings and sculptures (including works by Matisse, Bonnard and Picabia) from the Grammont collection. From the Ponche quarter, go up to the Citadel, dominated by a 16th century hexagonal tower ringed by three more towers and surrounded by a boundary wall built in the 17th century, where you can enjoy one of the most spectacular views of the city and the gulf. The Musée de la Marine, located inside the Citadel, includes objects and documents on the maritime history of Saint-Tropez.

1) The yearly Bravade commemorates the defense of St. Tropez against the Spanish fleet in 1637
2) La Ponche
3) Sunset

RAMATUELLE

This enchanting Provençal village is nestled among the vineyards of the Saint-Tropez hinterland. Its Romanesque origins are evident from the structure of the houses, laid out to form a sort of boundary wall around the city, and in the picturesque network of streets, narrow and often steep, adorned by arches that flow into the beautiful central square. Two large beaches, Pampelonne and Tahiti, are located nearby.

4) Panorama

GASSIN

Less worldly and noisy than the other towns in the area, this gracious Provençal city is located at the foot of the highest peaks of the Maures range. Within its boundary walls is a Romanesque church distinguished by a modern cloister completed in the late 1960's. Gassin offers a splendid view of the inland mountains, the gulf of Saint-Tropez, the bay of Cavalaire and the islands of Hyères.

Gassin: panorama

LA CROIX-VALMER

The leading tourist resort of the splendid Corniche des Maures, this beautiful vacation town owes its name to a legend that holds that this is where the emperor Constantine saw a vision of the cross bearing the phrase "In hoc signo vinces", an omen of his victory and conversion to Christianity. Near the city, which is also renowned for its high quality wines, the Col de Collebasse offers splendid panoramic views.

Croix Valmer: the beach

Sheltered by the crown of peaks of the Pradels mountains, the long beach of this pleasant swimming resort is quite popular due to its particularly fine sand.

The town is located at the tip of the bay of Cavalaire, which is closed off by Cap Lardier on the other side and overlooked by the buttresses of the Maures range inland.

In summer, a ferry service connects the town to the islands of Hyères.

The port and panorama

This small fishing port, a departure point for ferries traveling to the islands of Hyères, is located at the western end of Corniche des Maures, a short distance from Cap Bénat. The gracious residences in Provençal style and the modern hotel complexes are mirrored in the waters of the bay of Bormes, and here as well there are beautiful beaches of fine sand.

Le Lavandou: the well-known tourist resort at the tip of the bay of Bormes

At the edge of the lush forest of Dom, this town is situated at the foot of the slopes of the Maures range. This town is popular not only due to its excellent position, but also because of the beauty of the gardens that surround it, brimming with eucalyptus, oleander and, as its name hints, mimosas, which during the flowering season form a brightly colored crown for the picturesque town. The older part of the town is distinctively Provençal in character with its narrow, often steep streets, and boasts monuments such as the 16th century Chapelle de Saint-François, in front of which a scenic terrace offers a splendid view of the bay of Bormes. Near the church of Saint-Trophime (18th century), a street leads to the medieval castle of the lords of Fos. The Musée d'Arts et Histoire offers beautiful collections of works by landscape artists.

1) View
2) Picturesque corner

2

BORMES-LES-MIMOSAS

1) The fortress of Brègançon
2) La Favière: picturesque scene
3) La Faviere: aerial view
4) Cap-Bénat: Philippe Harbor

INDEX

© **KINA ITALIA** S.p.A. - Milan
Text: Claudia Converso
Layout: Renzo Matino - Schio
Printing: KINA ITALIA S.p.A. - Milan
Translations: A.B.A. - Milan
Photographs: F. Carlicchi Edition MAR